AUTHOR

A True Story

Happy 8th Birthday
Bret!
♡
Helen Lester

HELEN LESTER

HOUGHTON MIFFLIN COMPANY BOSTON

Walter Lorraine 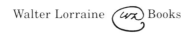 Books

Library of Congress Cataloging-in-Publication Data

Lester, Helen.
 Author: a true story / by Helen Lester.
   p.   cm.
 Summary: Children's author Helen Lester describes her life from
age three to adulthood and discusses how she writes.
 ISBN 0-395-82744-2
 1. Lester, Helen—Biography—Juvenile literature.   2. Women
authors, American—20th century—Biography—Juvenile literature.
3. Children's stories—Authorship—Juvenile literature.   4. Learning
disabled—Biography—Juvenile literature.   [1. Lester, Helen.
2. Authors, American. 3. Women—Biography.   4. Authorship.
5. Learning disabilities.]   I. Title.
PS3562.E8528A94   1997
813' .54
[B]—DC20   96-9645
                                                             CIP
                                                             AC

For information about this and other
Houghton Mifflin trade and reference books and
multimedia products, visit The Bookstore at
Houghton Mifflin on the World Wide Web at
http://www.hmco.com/trade/.

Printed in Singapore
TWP   10   9   8   7   6   5

For Robin, my husband and best friend

A long time ago there lived a three-year-old author.
Me.
I was the best groccry-list writer in the world
and a huge help to my mother.

When I wrote a word I knew <u>exactly</u> what it said.

And the fun part was that I could turn each list upside down and the words said the same thing.

I think I made hundreds of these useful lists
for my mother, and she never once said,
"No thank you, dear, I have enough."

Then I went to school and learned to make what they called "real letters."
My writing was the prettiest in the class, with straight straight lines and round round lines.
It was perfect.
And it was perfectly backwards.

I didn't just mix up b's and d's.
That's easy to do because they look so much alike.
My letters started at the right (well, wrong) side of the
paper and marched across, pretty as could be —
and backwards.

There's a name for somebody
with this problem.
I was a "mirror writer."
My teachers had to hold
my work up to a mirror
to understand what I
had written.

Thanks to a lot of help, I was finally able
to write in the proper direction.
But writing stories was so HARD for me!

Often I couldn't come up with a single idea,
and my stories got stuck in the middle,
and I couldn't think of a title,
and I had trouble making the changes my teacher
wanted me to make,
and I lost my pencils,
and I wondered why I was doing this,
and I got very very VERY frustrated.

So I spent a lot of time dreaming about
what I wanted to be when I grew up.

Since no one from the circus came looking for me,
I became a teacher.
I learned that teachers do not live in schools,
eating only crackers and milk and sleeping
under their desks.

I also learned that teaching was fun
and that children have fantastic imaginations.
So my favorite subject to teach was — writing!

One day a friend said, "You should write a children's book."

And I thought,
"I spent ten years in second grade,
so I know a child from a chicken.
Maybe I should."

I went right home and
wrote a book. It was
the best book I had
ever written.
Of course, it was the only
book I had ever written.

I illustrated it with my nicest drawings and
proudly sent it
to a publisher.
"Lucky people,"
I thought.

The lucky people sent it back and said, "No thank you."
That's called a rejection.
I decided I'd never write again.

Until the next day, when I felt better.
I wrote a second book and sent it to a different publisher.
The second publisher sent the book back. "No thank you."
I decided I'd never write again.
Until the next day, when I felt better.
I wrote another book.

And another.
And another.
And another.

Practice must have helped each story get a little
better, for on my seventh try no book came back.
Just a "Yes please."
That's called an acceptance.

I was beside myself with joy and excitement.
I was the first author I had ever met.

I drew the pictures for my first book.
And I did the pictures for this book.
But usually I work with an illustrator who has
been to art school and who can draw bicycles
and refrigerators and pigs.
This talented person draws what I would if I could.

MY PIG

MY ILLUSTRATOR'S PIG

So here I am. An author!
And every time I sit down to write, perfect
words line up in perfect order and WHOOP —
a perfect book pops out of the computer.

Well, not exactly.
Sometimes writing stories is so HARD for me!
I can't come up with a single idea,
and my stories get stuck in the middle,
and I can't think of a title,
and I have trouble making the changes my
editor wants me to make,
and I lose my pencils,
and I wonder why I'm doing this,
and I get very very VERY frustrated.

But that's sometimes.
I love it best when ideas are hatching so fast
I can barely write them down.
I grab the nearest thing to write on and get
so excited I forget what I was doing
in the first place.

The ideas that come
in the middle of the night
are hard to read the
next day.

Name that drawing!
How about one
two instead!
Possible ending + the
in the swamp
What frog
Check p. ₂₂

Not all of the ideas are useful.
I keep a whole box full of fizzled thoughts and
half-finished books. I call it my Fizzle Box.
Whenever I need an idea, I can go to the box
and find wonderful things — just the name I needed!
— a funny word!
— a wise lesson!

Usually when I first think a book
is finished, it really isn't.
I keep going over the story
again and again, looking for ways
to make it better with little
changes here and there. I do
this until the book has to be
printed. Then it's too late to
do anything more!

The Curious Rodent

~~The rodent was curious.~~ Nope. The rodent trembled with curiosity from his tail. to ~~his~~ <u>OR</u> how about? The rodents' head was stuck in a bag. Could his curiosity have led to this? ? ? ?

I used to think that writing had to be done
at a special time, while sitting at a desk.
But slowly I discovered that I could write
anytime.
And anywhere.
I especially like to write when I'm bored,
because then I'm not anymore.

Of course, writing anyTIME anyWHERE sometimes means writing on anyTHING.

Authors are lucky, for they get to meet
hundreds of children through letters, school
and library visits, and at autographing
sessions.
I didn't always like autographing books.
The first time I autographed, my table
was next to the table of a very famous
author.
I was not a very famous author.

Her line had no end.   Mine had no beginning.

I'm glad I didn't join the circus.
Even though writing is sometimes hard work,
it's what I love to do.
I never dreamed I'd become an author.
So this is better than a dream come true.